T0370416

IMAGINE YOU HAVE IT

It Will Show Up!

Dr. John D. McConnell

authorHOUSE®

AuthorHouse™
1663 Liberty Drive
Bloomington, IN 47403
www.authorhouse.com
Phone: 833-262-8899

Published by AuthorHouse 04/18/2024

ISBN: 979-8-8230-2414-3 (sc)
ISBN: 979-8-8230-2413-6 (e)

Library of Congress Control Number: 2024905788

Print information available on the last page.

CONTENTS

DEDICATION

I wouldn't be the free thinker I am today without those who've challenged me to hope for a good future. Family members, friends, educators, pastors – thank you for inspirational lessons that to this very day, provoke me to demand more for and from myself. Your investment in me taught me to invest in myself and others. I understand that circumstances in life are tests to reveal what we're really made of. Thank you to everyone who told me my worth, even before I discovered it for myself. I dedicate this book to all of you who never let me give up on my aspirations. Thanks for lighting my path and telling me the great things you saw within me. My dreams have not always been the most elaborate, but I thank God I have the ability to dream. My imagination has taken me so many places I've not yet stood, but because I have hope, I'm still in pursuit! I am continually evolving to become my best self, and that journey will not end until I've drawn my last breath. I am better because of my relationships (past, present, and future). I pray I've not taken more than I've given - and that you feel just as edified having had me as part of your lives. My prayer for you all is to never be limited by your imaginations but lifted far above them.

INTRODUCTION

Imagine you have it. It's yours, but you must see yourself with it first. As kids, we all were snapped back into reality multiple times with the phrase, "Stop daydreaming!" As it turns out, daydreaming is the solution to getting what you really want in life. The daydream is the placeholder for the prize. No one gets harmed.

The human brain can generate about 23 watts of power (enough to power a lightbulb). Brain scan studies have repeatedly found that seeing something and imagining it evoke highly similar patterns of neural activity. Saying it another way – Our brain sees what's in our imagination as being just as real as something in our hand. I am challenged with diabetic retinopathy, which involves blood vessels that have formed to cover much of my center of vision. Low vision specialists have assisted me with strategies for reading lines of information that my eyes can't completely see. The brain fills in for the missing puzzle pieces. This is called 'convergence'. Your eye and brain carefully coordinate these changes. The result is that you can see a single focused image. When you read, your eyes and brain must coordinate the quick complex eye movements needed to scan a page. It's time we tap into the processing power of our brain and allow it to partner with our imagination. It's an actual superpower we all have access to. It's important that we use our power cautiously. It takes just as much energy to imagine "bad" as it does to imagine "good". We already know that there's much power in our words. The things we consistently say about ourselves, we begin to believe, and ultimately start to see. Role-playing a drama in your mind works the same way. Cast yourself in the lead role. Add the most positive dialogue and play it in your mind on a continuous loop. Whatever it is you want to bring into your life, you must resolutely IMAGINE YOU HAVE IT!!

CHAPTER 1

ATTITUDE DETERMINES ALTITUDE

No one has more say in how powerful your voice is than you. I know that's very different from what you've been hearing. Your voice might not be heard by nearly as many people as someone else's, but that does not negate its power. Not understanding the difference could cause you to devalue what you have to say. Whether your audience is just the three people who live in your house, or the six hundred fifty-three people you supervise at work, what you speak is valuable. Always remain cognizant of this fact, so you won't waste words. Even if no one ever reads or hears words I've written, at the very least, I am the one strengthened just from planting. Your exposure to my words alter your thoughts; they spill over into your life. With or without an audience, I have influence. Anything you want to do in life begins with a decision, and a decision starts with a seed.

It's not a difficult feat to be negative. Negativity is all around us. We are conditioned to believe that positivity can only show up as a result of overpowering an already existing negative force. Our highest regarded children's books embolden the message that a big bad wolf is necessary to influence the construction of a fortified home. A wicked stepmother is required in order for Cinderella to win the battle of good versus evil. A princess must first kiss a frog before her prince is released from

2   *Dr. John D. McConnell*

the spell of a wicked witch. In most stories, the protagonist is not celebrated without there first being an antagonist (adversary) to overcome. If this is what we learn as children, no wonder using our imagination for good is such a chore. Even in music, many popular rap artists are incorporating their experiences with anxiety, depression, and PTSD into their lyrics. Culture experts believe these messages will help to remove the stigma from mental health, and encourage more people to seek help for their disorders. These issues extend far beyond the hip-hop community. Beyond race, age, or gender, battling negative identities affect the global community. Bad doesn't always precede good. If we will start reversing the way we teach it, our children won't see good as the underdog - but the favorite to win. Let's stop allowing negativity to be the loudest and most dominant. Characterize negativity as having the voice of a whisper. After all, it's only true power is suggestion. If we stop giving negativity so much equity, its value will tank, shrivel, and disappear.

The miracle these days is to approach people and situations with positivity. Not allowing the bad things that happened to derail your current climb is truly hard - but not impossible. Every day let's purpose to find the joy in our journey. If you've been sidelined and exhausted by life's pressures, finding the joy won't come easy. You must; however, bring joy to everything you do. Joy is to achievement as the principle of lift is to an airplane. You are subject to crash and burn without it. We always hear about the importance of a good diet, exercise, and the proper amount of sleep. What's not usually mentioned is that the consistent messaging we receive will determine whether we soar or plummet. It's not organic for all people

 Dr. John D. McConnell

to have a "natural curiosity", or a vivid imagination. Have you ever met someone who seemed completely void of aspiration? There are many reasons people stop believing for more, but a portion of them were never taught how to dream. Depending on when and where you were raised, your imagination may never have been required. If you ever walk into an elementary school classroom, you'll notice positive affirmations and quotes along the walls. "The power to win comes from within." "If you can see it, you can be it." "You must read to succeed." "The only way to win a race is to never stop running." This type of messaging is seed for the soul. I read it every day, and it was spoken to me as a child. Positive messaging was like a daily vitamin I received from all the adults I spent time around. It was injected encouragement, which made imagining myself thriving easy to do. I realize that's my story, and not all people share that experience. Most of us, however, can recall this type of motivation as a child.

WHAT DO YOU BELIEVE?

No matter where you're receiving your messaging, it will only confirm or challenge what you already believe. Most belief systems' foundation come solely from how we are raised (taught, nurtured). Our behaviors and ideologies are instilled by who and what immediately surrounds us. To adopt routines outside of "the norm" puts a target on your back. Pardon the idiom, but 'you stick out like a sore thumb'. For one person to challenge a belief held by many, comes off as combative. If we simply conform to who we're told to be, what does that say about us? I'm not suggesting that the popular opinion isn't always the right one. I'm suggesting that it might not always be right for you. Do you have a "herd mentality", and choose the direction everybody runs? Or do you have a process for arriving at how you believe? If you apply critical thinking strategies for every decision you make, the more messaging that comes in, will be filtered accordingly.

From where are you receiving your messaging as an adult? It's still important. The market size measured by revenue of the advertising agencies industry in the US was $68.4 billion in 2022. The correlation between suggestions for how you should spend your money, and actual purchases is well documented. It's been proven that millions of people are persuaded by commercials of how they should think, look, talk, walk, live, and drive. Don't think of it all as unsolicited brainwashing. Google and YouTube searches confirm that people are actually asking how to kiss, vacation, apply makeup, etc. Solicited or unsolicited, we are all impacted today by an abundance of messaging. If we're not cautious, we could very easily stop thinking for ourselves. I hope this book will incentivize you to at least consider why you think the way you do. Do you really have an imagination, or are you trying to bring someone else's dream into your reality?

What you allow to penetrate your ears, your eyes, and escape from your mouth determines what you believe. Anything we make consistent and habitual begins taking root. We transition from questioning to believing. Once something becomes part of our belief system, those roots spread and run deep.

It's during times of despair that I find I need my imagination most. I had this pattern of complaining during frustration. It's always been easy to recognize external sources as the culprit, rather than owning my own stuff. Even when no one was at fault for what occurred, it felt better to assign blame. I had to challenge that thinking. That's just not right. I am learning to allow things to breathe. Everything doesn't necessitate an immediate response. Before sending the text or making the phone call, I remove myself from the situation. When I can't physically employ distance, I imagine the scenario being resolved. This allows me to breathe, calm down, and develop an intentional response. As long as we have our imagination, any circumstance that does not cause death is rectifiable. My imagination provides a substitute solution until the hard copy shows up. Living this way provides me with so many benefits. Clearly it supports my stress management. Reimagining before responding supports the integrity of my interpersonal relationships. I'm less likely to have to apologize for losing control if I never lose control. People also admire one's ability to stay even keel when surrounded by chaos.

A good night's sleep for me is heavily dependent upon what's on my mind when my head hits the pillow. When emotions like worry and anger come to bed with you, it's a set up for tossing and turning. The mind becomes fixated on what you're thinking about the most.

Sleep study data contends that we spend about two hours each night dreaming but may not remember most of our dreams. The exact purpose of dreams is unknown, but dreaming may help us process our emotions. Events from the day often invade our thoughts during sleep, and people suffering from stress or anxiety are more likely to have frightening dreams. We power down at night, but the brain never actually switches off.

Dr. John D. McConnell

HOW DO GOOD THOUGHTS IMPACT SLEEP?

Repeating the same positive thought over and over to yourself allows you to release the stresses of your day, and relax to sleep. I don't believe it's possible to consistently repeat something and never begin to formulate an image in your mind. What we write down turns into the words we say. What we say legitimizes what we begin to imagine. The more vividly a person imagines something, the more likely it is they believe it's real.

What if instead of always hovering near the ground, you talked yourself into a much higher elevation? Would your life be dramatically different if you were unable to see failure as an option? Imagine you have it!

CHAPTER 2

LET THE LOVE IN

How are you with being loved? Can love only visit you, or do you allow it to stay? If you don't feel deserving of what someone tries to give, it will never really be yours. When you spend so much time trying to answer how something arrived, unintentionally you can push it away - never regarding it as being for you. It's almost impossible to reciprocate feelings we don't believe we are entitled to. I am asking you to pivot and try to view things through a different perspective. You can't give what you don't have, so you must find ways to retain love.

What initially causes someone to be captivated by you may have nothing to do with anything you can control. It could happen on what you may perceive as your worst day. Stopping someone from becoming intrigued is impossible. The decision one makes to come closer and pursue partly relies on you. Although inclusive, this is a broader topic than just romantic relationships. You may appeal to a particular brand or corporation. Someone could decide that you have the voice they want to represent their product globally. There are things about you that others find to be magnetic, and you have no clue why. Someone is always watching, and we don't always get to decide where the invitation will come from. But just as sure as people can be drawn to you, they can also be repelled by you. Not everyone will fight to love you. Even those with the most impenetrable shell must allow access if someone is to ever risk getting close. Those who constantly drive people away, remain alone. There is a heightened potential for bad things to occur in our lives due to being alone. No matter what you have going for you that entices people to come your way, if you never learn how to be a friend, they will always leave. There is an art to being a friend that I am still trying to tap into, because I realize how valuable good friendships truly are. Begin imagining stronger, healthier relationships for yourself.

Emotions can be misinterpreted. Everything we call love isn't love. Displaying emotions and labeling them are two different things. You may believe you're displaying empathy towards me when what you're actually displaying is sympathy. An empathetic heart recognizes and relates to someone's pain, whereas someone offering sympathy may have never faced your reality.

Dr. John D. McConnell

It changes everything. It doesn't mean you don't care as much. But it means you've never been where I am. Expectations are tied to the emotions we label. We may enjoy a very strong, mutual connection, which makes us feel safe in each other's presence. If it's the closest relationship you've ever experienced, you may be quick to label it as love. Love is deeper. It's unselfish and makes one sacrifice for the other. How much you have to ask of someone will help you determine if love is the appropriate label.

Just because you're able to show love, doesn't make you a great candidate to receive it. Our past plays a huge role in how intimate we allow ourselves to be going forward. It's important to acknowledge the scars we carry. Some wounds don't just heal on their own. If someone has mishandled your heart in the past, it can be traumatic. Life has so much more to offer on the other side of healing. Don't succumb to a life absent of love. If you've talked yourself out of ever being loved again, the conversation should be re-initiated. It's my opinion that we love others better when we are recipients of love. It's like a bucket under a water faucet. Once the water reaches the top, it has no choice, but to spill over onto everything in its proximity. Fight the barriers of embarrassment, fatigue, and low self-esteem to become whole again. Don't ignore your emotions. Just be careful to label them properly so your expectations of others are fair.

I invited a woman to dinner whom I had been admiring from afar. As we received our menus, I began telling her all the things that made me want to spend time with her. She placed her hand on her chest, and in a soft, modest voice she said, "me?" She was so flattered, and it was cute how unsuspecting she was that I was talking about her attributes.

This posture continued throughout the meal. With each complement I offered, she kept responding exactly the same way. It was almost like it was too big for her to receive. I could see her mind trying to decide whether or not to own it.

We are multi-dimensional beings and our effect on people will not always be the same. That's a good thing. It doesn't mean that all people will see us the way we want to be seen. People have different motives in how they choose to perceive us. Our responsibility is to embrace what's accurate and positive about how we're viewed, and be intentional about not perpetuating the inaccuracies.

I mentioned earlier that even without attempting to do so, there are qualities we have that attract - like a moth to a bright light. No one in this world is without attraction. Makeover shows have demonstrated that we can do things to bump our attraction up a whole new level. TV shows like "Dream Home Makeover", "Bar Rescue", "Undercover Boss", and "Iyanla Vanzant's Fix My Life" focus on making something that's attractive, even more attractive. There's nothing wrong with trying to present the very best version of ourselves, our homes, businesses, etc. If someone is already attracted to you, making improvements only intensifies the attraction.

We can imagine for increased attraction when we recognize that we are attractive. But where does that leave people who have not recognized their attraction? Imagining awesome things entering your life is difficult when you don't feel attractive. There are things that seem out of reach. Not only are they light years away, but when you see flashes of great things happening, it's not your face you picture. It's quirky how it's easier for us to imagine great things for other people, but not for ourselves. Until you can see it for you, there's no way to expect it to come. Before you can call it in with your voice, you must first see it in your mind. Think it for you! Attract it to invade your life. The more you ponder a thought, the more you increase its attraction to you. Your expectation will eventually become manifestation.

Everything we experience leaves a mark. Some are more visible than others. We choose which ones to flaunt as badges of honor, while trying desperately to keep others hidden. It's normal to have days, months, or even years we're not proud of. Instead of acting like it didn't happen, celebrate surviving it and imagine something better. What has you marked? Are there any labels you're trying to shed? It's really difficult to live your truth while spending so much time in hiding. I was an obese kid growing up suffering from Tourette's Syndrome. I had these ticks that caused me to rapidly shake my head and violently blink my eyes. It wouldn't happen all the time, but I wasn't in control of it. I spent so much energy trying to avert attention away from myself, while unintentionally pulling it towards me. I wore masks to deflect the fat jokes and created stories for the ticks. I remember circle-time in Mrs. Nesby's third grade classroom. A classmate noticed my antics. He whispered, "Why do you do that?" I told him it was a game I play. "I catch a fly under my eyelid, then I shake it loose". I really wanted to escape the world I was living in, and my imagination was trying to do its part. I was bullied a lot, but somehow it never got the starring role it was seeking. I suffered from low self-esteem but was never submerged by it. It took several years for me to finally realize the body type I had imagined for so long. Some things we imagine for our lives are delayed. Sacrifices and hard work is required in many cases.

When your imagination is at work, don't allow the daydream to end before it shows you strategies and steps for getting there.

I know people who work overtime to ensure a certain reputation. On some level, we all are curious regarding the stories being scripted about us. Even without being able to control the narrative, hours of creative thought-time are exchanged for worry. Labels are meaningless unless or until you buy-in to them.

What would your life be like if you were receptive to people and situations pouring into you? How awesome would it feel to be able to move past skepticism, and respond to love with love? Imagine you have it!

CHAPTER 3

JUST RIGHT FOR ME

Don't hang your imagination out to dry. It needs your participation. It's illogical to rely only upon your thoughts to manufacture your world. Having the ability to think it is a key component, but we must run towards what we're imagining while believing it's racing towards us. Embarrassment is an acquired taste. I know that sounds horrible. No one enjoys the feeling of being embarrassed. I am referring to the private embarrassment that some call conviction. We've all experienced it. It's when you go back for three additional cookies when your plan was to only have one, or when you put your Fitbit on your dog's collar and count those steps as your own. Only you know about it, and you'd never consider those your finest moments. Get chummy with that feeling so it can be what forces you to confront demanding the best from and for yourself. It wasn't private embarrassment that slowed us from going hard, but the deflated feelings of failure as children set the tone. Think back to tryouts for the sports team, the school play, choir, band, etc. Now, those results are posted online. Back in my day you had to read it from a list posted on a bulletin board. I don't know which was worse. Not finding your name on the list hurts in any format. We took the risk and placed ourselves on exhibition to only be shot down. Optimism forces you to rewrite the story differently in your mind, but the facts of those encounters actually occurred. How many times can the most optimistic person willingly stand before the firing squad? For some of us, we know exactly when the shutdown occurred. I have not written this book in an attempt to talk you into re-opening old wounds. I am encouraging you to no longer allow how you've been conditioned to think to rule your choices.

Choose your desires based on them being just right for you. Only you get to decide that. We nurture our trauma when we rehearse the same script from the past. Believing you'll meet rejection will cause you to retreat every time. You must believe something else. Your reasons for why it's just right for you is enough. What you want may be far removed from anything anyone in your family has ever done. That's what transformative thinking is. It goes beyond the mundane. Box-thinkers will always try to reel you back in because they can't comprehend what you're believing for. If you don't apply for the position, the bank loan, or the grant, you

Dr. John D. McConnell

will never receive it. It's not magic. There is obviously a process for acquiring certain things. Fear has an acronym (false evidence appearing real). Don't be afraid of "no". It's simply means "not yet".

Don't allow yourself to become a passive victim. Not long ago, I booked a flight to travel from Houston to Chicago. I completed my booking three months early because I was particular about securing a direct flight with no layovers. On two occasions as the trip got closer, the airline emailed me that flight schedules had changed, and prompted me to accept new flight itineraries. After having a chance to thoroughly review what I had accepted, I noticed that I went from having a two-hour direct flight to having a ten-hour trip (flying from Houston to Orlando, debarking for a four-hour layover, changing planes, and flying two more hours to Chicago). I almost did nothing about it. The defeated victim in me said, "Surely they offered you the most comparable itinerary available - and after all, you did click to accept the modification". Over the next few days, it kept coming up in my thinking that I deserved more. I imagined how I'd feel leaving Houston at 7 AM and not arriving in Chicago until 5 PM. That's literally not what I signed up for. That travel plan is not just right for me. I was embarrassed for myself being in this situation without pushing back. I determined that my hesitation in calling customer service was connected to feeling my request for a better flight would be rejected. It took five days to deliberate over what a five-minute phone conversation solved. I thoroughly explained the situation, and my desire to a customer service representative, and they kindly made the adjustments on my behalf - securing a two-hour direct flight from Houston to Chicago. Begin speaking up for what you deserve. Allow those victories to build your confidence to believe more for what you want.

Destiny cannot be stripped away from us. We can; however, pollute the path with noise and clutter, that will keep it hidden. We long to find that moment in life where everything makes sense. The reason we were misunderstood in relationships, or why every job was the wrong one - can all finally be explained. Will finally ever come? Why do some see it, and others don't? To "make your way prosperous" doesn't always mean you should constantly stay busy. The quote "Idle hands are the devil's workshop" is an example of counterproductive messaging. In theory, it means you're more likely to gravitate towards trouble if your time isn't already committed to productive things. While it can be viewed as a strategy for making progress, it also commends always being busy. Everything in life requires balance. As a kid, I watched girls playing

Double Dutch on the school playground. This is a game in which two long jump ropes turning in opposite directions, are jumped by one or more players, jumping simultaneously. The girls who were great at it understood that the ropes must be turning before the jumper can successfully enter. There is a rhythm to how the ropes are being turned. If the jumpers don't match that rhythm before jumping in, the ropes will always hit their legs. Many of us are being hit by the ropes because we won't respect the rhythm of life. You cannot force a destiny that's not yours. Acquiring a lifestyle you've chased for years won't necessarily equate to you living your destiny. If what you amass does not come with fulfillment, it's not destiny. Coaches are celebrated when the plays they've designed result in victory. Are you correctly hearing your play calls? Are you in the right position for how the defense is aligned? If you're making decisions that are alienating you from your harvest, you must identify who or what is in the coach's seat.

Many have become the epitome of their mind's creation. Unfortunately, the potter's wheel of most mindsets is malnourished and war fatigued. How does one not grow accustomed to low expectations when only poverty and despair are on the menu? If what they say is true, that "we are what we eat", a large number of people are functioning way below the line. On a steady diet of hope and belief, the mind can grow wings. Begin with something relatively simple, like paying off a debt. Create a monthly plan for how much you will pay, and do it consistently. This will activate your intention. Once the debt reaches zero dollars, it gives birth to pride. You begin having a sense of accomplishment where you never had it before. Because of how we're built, your pleasure center will seek to repeat that action and feel that feeling again and again. Your mind is learning to imagine your debts being paid. Each victory stretches the imagination for more vivid images of grandiose accomplishments.

The world we know of is just that. But what about the things we've not yet experienced? How do they get to be part of what we acknowledge as the human experience? Who will be the next Charles Babbage, Albert Einstein, Charles Darwin, Stephen Hawking, or Richard Feynman? What is hidden within you that the entire world could benefit from? Your imagination is the key. It holds treasures of new inventions, songs, books, and maybe even the cure for cancer.

Our fleeting thoughts and actions of today, may prove to be invaluable in their proper season. When we're looking for results that matter most, the timing is important. Although we can't control time, we can offer ideas.

 Dr. John D. McConnell

I've always loved this poem by Henry Wadsworth Longfellow:

"The Arrow and The Song"

I shot an arrow into the air. It fell to earth I knew not where, for so swiftly it flew the site could not follow it in its flight. I breathed a song into the air. It fell to earth I knew not where, for who has sight so keen and strong that it can follow the flight of song Long, long afterward in an oak, I found the arrow still unbroke and song from beginning to end, I found again in the heart of a friend.

I believe this poem acts as a metaphor, depicting the results of one's actions, specifically those that are momentary or non-physical. To me it illustrates someone identifying something they want and taking their shot. The arrow totally missed and yielded a zero return. But the song made a connection and brought back a friend. Furthermore, it suggests that we must be flexible and aggressive enough to have more than one strategy for our pursuit. That's how our imagination gives us an assist.

Do you think you would feel more self-actualized if you were living the life that's just right for you? Are you ready to not rely on optimism as a substitute for manifestation? Imagine You Have It!

CHAPTER 4

PARENTING BEYOND EXPECTATION

After coping with thwarted childhood dreams, we press on with a desire to be a good companion to who we choose to partner our lives, hoping ultimately to become good parents. I had the marriage I first imagined for many years. Our children were born into the most loving, nurturing environment. It's uncanny how the thing you work so hard to never imagine for your life can show up and completely re-define it. I don't fully understand how two people who chose one another for life can spiral and hurt each other to the point of disconnection - but it happened to us. My sons were age fifteen and thirteen when the marriage ended. This is significant to me for so many reasons. I remember myself at this age transitioning from middle school to high school. I recall feeling so unsure of myself. I would go to my dad for my swagger and to my mom for my confidence. I found it difficult to keep up with how fast my world was changing. At fifteen I won a spot on the freshman basketball team, attended my first dance, and experienced my first kiss. My dad got the names, but my mom got the details. I'm not saying that my sons' mother was out of the picture, but she was no longer living with us. The casual quick check-in conversations during breakfast before catching the bus to school, and while clearing the table following dinner, were no longer options for them. Those connections had to become more intentional, and I just didn't see it. I felt pressure to be more maternal for them, but of course I didn't know how. I realize that we all have different experiences, and that I shouldn't assume my sons needed the same reinforcements I received growing up. When I think about how valuable that support system was for me at that age, naturally, I want to shroud my kids with that same nurturing. For me to make it, I needed my mom to be physically close. She and my dad had totally different roles, and there's no way he could've guided me through my stuff by himself. It felt like I had her undivided attention during those years. That's absolutely amazing, especially since I had five other siblings who felt the same way.

My mother's approval meant everything to me, from childhood, until the day she passed in 2006. I always knew where my mom stood regarding my choices, and that was just fine with me. She was like a barometer. I'd check with her before making big decisions. She showed up for anything school-related, and I particularly recall a fourth-grade memory. One morning at Quindaro Elementary, Mrs. Berry, my fourth-grade teacher, announced that we were having a special assembly. As our class reached the bottom landing of the stairs, the elevator doors opened, and my mom stepped out with the school principal and district superintendent. I remember thinking, "What is she doing here?" As the entire student body filed into the music room, I noticed no other parents were there. Usually, the school assemblies occurred in the cafeteria, which allowed plenty of room for family members. My eyes were trained on her as she walked in and sat in a reserved seat near the front. "What have I done?", I thought. "I know I'm not in trouble because she's smiling and waving at me". My mind was racing to discover what this moment was about. Dr. Orvin L. Plucker announced himself as the district superintendent. He said the purpose of the assembly was to celebrate one student for outperforming all fourth-grade students throughout the twenty-five elementary schools in a writing competition. "I am congratulating John David McConnell as the winner of this year's writing competition for his paper on the Industrial Revolution". I was awarded a bronze medal, which was pinned on me by my mother. The entire room erupted with celebratory applause and cheers. My mom's tears, contagious as chickenpox, spread to my tear ducts as she hugged me ever so tight with approval. I have never wanted to be absent of that approval. Since that day, imagining ways to impress my mom became a quest. I came to learn that my happiness was not only my own, but also those rooting for me. Not everyone can say with absolution, they know who's on their team. Who can say just how many external forces are responsible for powering our imaginations? Forty-six years have passed since fourth grade, and seventeen years since she died. Yet, every decision I make is funneled through the mom filter. Just because she's not physically here, doesn't mean I'm free to forsake choices she would honor. I'm not imprisoned by her memory, but morally guided because of it.

My kids are now in their twenties, and even with all the disconnect that occurred as a result of divorce, I have well-rounded, amazing, respectful, confident young men. I have always imagined my children having the opportunities to display integrity and good character. I have imagined them thriving in their most tedious endeavors. God empowered their mom and I to parent them through the turbulence, and I am in awe that we did not wreck their lives. Imagine greatness for your kids. Speak favor over their lives. They're only on loan to us from God until He reveals to them their purpose; so let's be the best stewards we can be.

I was a surrogate father (of sorts) for hundreds of kids during my twenty-seven years as a schoolteacher. If you genuinely make yourself available, God will cause your life to intersect with kids when they need it most. When kids don't know how to imagine a better life for themselves, begin to imagine for them. Show them who they can be through your example. Mentor them through their insecurities by introducing them to biographies and autobiographies of winners who look like them. We can't always control the timing of being in someone's life. Think about the people who've made valuable deposits in you. We hold those memories because of how they shifted us to the path we needed to be on. Sometimes it's not the people who choose us, but the moments.

On my next birthday, I'll be the age my dad was when he died. It seems like only yesterday, but thirty-four years have come and gone. Most of what he taught me was informal. I got it by paying attention – watching him live. I never compared him to other dads, privately hoping he'd be better. In my eyes, he was the best - always honoring his commitments. Mine was a blue-collar dad who worked really hard. On Sundays, Mr. Blue-collar traded up for three-piece suits as a treasurer and the chairman of our church's deacon board. As a weekday school janitor, and weekend church officer, he was highly respected. My father's example taught me that it's not the position that earns a man respect, but the way a man functions in a position. Because of his and my mom's work ethic, the tone was set early in our house that there would be no slackers. My parents didn't make us work. They did something much more powerful – they set the expectations. Even today, I don't argue with my sons about low productivity. Instead, I make sure that my expectations of them have been clearly communicated. I don't want my children to do what I tell them to do, as much as wanting them to abhor disappointing me. Some kids could care less whether they disappoint their parents. Pause a moment from reading to ask your children where they stand. You may be shocked by their answer. Although my life is mine to live, it's always been important to me to represent my family well. As you're reading this book, don't only read it for what you can gain, but for what you can give. All those you influence, perhaps see you as their standard. No matter their connection to you, live well before them. Take away their excuses for giving up by never allowing them to see you throw in the towel. Apprehending the most distinguished honors means very little if the path you took was corrupt and unconscionable. It's better to go hard after something with your morality intact, and not get it - than it is to reach the peak, having lost all integrity. I believe the reason my imagination works for me is because I submitted my life to people who never took it for granted. The earlier in life you learn that people are taking steps based on yours, the sooner you stop allowing defeat to be an option.

"All of my battles, I won't see the end – but through my example, those battles my children will win!"

Do you believe you are equipped to successfully parent children in the world we live in today? Do you have the patience, wisdom, and knowledge to be a good parent? Imagine You Have It!

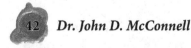

42   *Dr. John D. McConnell*

CHAPTER 5

RECOGNIZING PEACE

CAN YOU RECOGNIZE PEACE?

I do not subscribe to the belief that peace can only be attained once we go to the grave. For most people; however, peace never becomes part of their résumé. Everyone has a place of tranquility, but it's not a destination. It's not an official part of speech (yet), but I would call peace/tranquility, a noun-atude. It's a combination of being in the right place coupled with having the right attitude. Your place of tranquility won't necessarily resemble mine. A barrier to getting there is recognizing what it looks and feels like. How will you know when you're at peace? Not everyone has lived a life of privilege. There are some whose entire existence has been a fight. You've had to use persuasion just to be considered and valued since day one. No victories have been experienced without you having to prove yourself. Every job, promotion, or increase in pay arrived because of nothing short of a battle. Even those are short-lived, allowing you only moments before the next proving ground. Here's how powerful the imagination is. Even in the cycle of fighting for a good life, you have the ability to trick your mind for moments at a time to experience peace. It's called vacation.

My first vacation was a Carnival Cruise in 2001. Back then JC Penny had a travel services division, and I was able to book the cruise using my credit account. I spent the next six years settling the debt from that six-day vacation. We all make decisions based on the cards we are dealt. The key is to recognize when you're not playing the game successfully, and allow that to motivate you towards growth. As I reflect, I wouldn't classify my first few vacations as good, but necessary. Financially, I was increasing my debt with each transaction. But emotionally, those moments afforded me the opportunity to recharge and reset my focus for going forward. I would never validate unconscionable spending. I am simply making the point that the fruit of the purchase was necessary. An awesome thing that happens while vacationing is, you get to witness others who do it better than you. While you're renting a jet ski for your family of four to share for an hour, you intersect with another family, who each have their own jet ski for the entire day. It stings a little at first, but it stretches you to imagine for more. It's on vacation when we get glimpses of what peace and tranquility truly look like. If you are fortunate enough to be able to detach yourself from your normal flow of life while on vacation, all five of your senses will experience flashes of peace. Imagine what life would be like if you could find your place of peace and never have to let it go.

Creativity can easily be smoldered by the pressures of life. So many things confront families that easily distract from dreaming. Sluggishness and fatigue pile on in the absence of peace. How do you plug into imagination when there's no time to unplug from the grind that is reality? You may be thinking, "I can't afford to take a vacation". The truth is, you can't afford not to. If circumstances won't allow you to take a traditional vacation, you must figure out a way to shut out the noise – even if only for a little while. Having off duty time to meditate is a gift we should all give ourselves. Monday through Friday I wake up early, giving the first two hours of my day to exercise and meditation. Within my two hours, I pray, walk, and dictate my thoughts as notes on my phone. When I begin my days this way, I'm better poised to focus and prioritize. It's empowering to set the tone for your day, rather than becoming a victim of your day's flow. Of course I have negative situations that show up, but they don't disturb me nearly as much as when I'm mentally unprepared. Early mornings are when I experience my best thoughts. Over the span of months, the thoughts I dictate become paragraphs, then chapters, then books. That small amount of time I invest in myself each morning, rewards me with a product of immeasurable value. We all need moments of peace, because from peace, entire worlds are imagined. Carve out a consistent amount of time for yourself each week to turn off the flat-screen and your normal distractions. I know justifying that you have no extra time is easier than finding it. I also know that without becoming someone who uses his/her imagination, you will forever be a victim of what happens.

Happiness and contentment are not nearly the same, and you deserve a celebration if you are content with the person you see in the mirror every day. There is a large population of miserable people, due to the feeling of remorse. When they look in the mirror, they feel betrayed by who they've become. Are you tolerating things you once vowed to never allow to coexist in your life? Has your fear of change ripped holes in your sails? Being unhappy with ourselves sometimes attracts other things we don't want. We take on an attitude of defeat, and approach each day with almost no expectation of good. If you've ever fallen in a lake or pool fully dressed, you know how difficult it is to climb out of the water. Everything connected to you becomes an anchor, and makes movement nearly impossible. We must find a way to shed all of the heaviness clinging to keep us trapped. Neither peace nor great imaginations reside in dark places.

GOLDFISH IS TO LOW EXPECTATIONS AS TILAPIA IS TO A VIVID IMAGINATION.

Most fish live either in freshwater or saltwater. Goldfish mainly occupy fresh inland waters, wetlands, and temperate regions. They usually live in rivers, lakes, streams, ponds, bogs, marshes, and swamps with little to no movement.

Freshwater fish cannot survive in the ocean or saltwater. The sea water inside their bodies would cause their cells to shrivel and die of dehydration.

Tilapias have the remarkable ability to physiologically adjust to various salinity levels. This is a phenomenal trait, as climate change has begun altering the salinity of coastal and ocean waters.

The longer our imagination lies dormant, the harder it will be to flicker a flame. I know it's impossible to choose our own species, because if magic was real, we wouldn't need our imagination. Metaphorically, be the Tilapia, and thrive in both ponds and oceans. Maintain a healthy perception of who you are, without aborting hope of who you can be. Don't drown in an ever-changing world because of an inability to adapt.

It's fascinating that 71% of the earth's surface is water covered, and the oceans hold about 96.5% of all its water. Fish have a larger habitat on earth than human beings.

They've won that competition, hands-down. But what life-force has the ability to envision what lies below the ocean floor, and beyond our atmosphere? Wake up to these truths regarding your imagination. Your imagination gives you the ability to occupy a space your feet have yet to trod. With it, you can smell and taste cuisines you've not had the privilege to look upon. The imagination is a portal that will transport you to foreign lands without a passport. It's currency for what's not presently in your bank account or crypto wallet.

It's outside of the natural order for children to die before their parents. One of the reasons it's so difficult for parents is because we mourn the many milestones they will never accomplish. It's not a selfish type of mourning, for the expectations we had for them. But a grieving for the termination of goals they had for themselves. If that is a justifiable reason for grief, why do we have peace to stop progressing as adults when we reach a certain age? If it became a trend to mourn people in their seventies who have not accomplished their dreams, we'd feel more obligated to test the limits of our imagination until death. It's the hunt that keeps us alive.

Asia and Europe are home to some of the world's oldest populations - those ages sixty-five and above. Japan is at the top with 28%, followed by Italy at 23%. Finland, Portugal, and Greece round out the top five at just under 22%. The life expectancy in Japan is 84.62 years, and 77.28 years in the United States. Good healthcare, and a great diet are amongst the contributing factors for a lengthier lifespan amongst the people of Japan, but I'm sure a continued expectation of productivity also plays a part. No matter where you live, make it your focus to stay plugged in. People who delay retirement, maintain a higher level of mobility. That's because we have an innate ability to rise to meet the challenges we set for ourselves.

What if you discovered a way to remove time bandits from your life? How deliberate would you be in redeeming the time? If you could have a shorter workday, and double your productivity, would you leap at the opportunity? Imagine You Have It!

CHAPTER 6

TWO IMAGINING AS ONE

When I think of great acting duos, I think of Adam Sandler and Drew Barrymore, Jane Fonda and Lily Tomlin, Robert De Niro and Al Pacino, and Abbott and Costello. Great sports duos include Michael Jordan and Scottie Pippen, Babe Ruth, and Lou Gehrig, Magic Johnson and Kareem Abdul-Jabbar, Venus and Serena Williams, and Wayne Gretzky, and Mark Messer. Some famous cofounders include William Proctor and James Gamble, Bill Hewitt and Dave Packard,

Bill Gates and Paul Allen, and Steve Jobs and Steve Wozniak.

A shared imagination is what causes people to pledge their lives to one another. Whether it's a marriage, a business, team, or ministry, when people imagine it the same, there is a euphoria. It's more than being persuaded or buying in. The connection becomes as vital as breathing. When I was asked thirty-three years ago, how I knew it was the right time for me to get married, I responded, "I can no longer live without her because nothing else makes since. It physically hurts to not be in her presence every day." When people arrive at a joint imagination, it legitimizes the goal. It's a lot less risky to achieve if I have someone at my side, fighting for the exact same thing. The unity of the pursuit increases the likelihood of actually seeing the vision materialize. It's no longer one person scurrying for the energy to keep a dream afloat, but two. There is power in togetherness. Sometimes just feeling like you have camaraderie with others is enough to encourage you to make broad strokes toward imagining greatness. When people dream together, they become allies. Allies relish in stepping up for one another. As your ally, I'm right there with you to run interference for anything contrary to what we've imagined. When you're feeling weak, I apply my strength. When I am frustrated and combative, you calm me with soft words.

As a team, no one person is responsible for the productivity. More things get the attention they deserve when you're not working alone. Important elements are often overlooked when people who are not gifted in a certain area, try to do it all. Accomplishing tasks by committee is not a new concept, but collaborations worth bragging about are hard to come by. How you choose partners is just as important as who you choose. Your method or process of selection must be so much more than simply choosing people who choose you. Of course, having things in common matters. But what good is a room full of people with like philosophies, if not one is a critical thinker? It's imperative that diversity play a role when pulling people together. Imagining as one is simply one part of the collaboration recipe. Think of it in terms of a football team. If a team's offensive personnel consists of only quarterbacks, they will undoubtingly fail. Even with assembling the greatest quarterbacks to have ever played the game, you must have talented running backs to hand the ball off to, or great receivers to catch the ball. Without a way to successfully get the football into the endzone, your team has no way to score points. In this scenario, their ability to imagine as one is worthless. Choose people who choose you, but also choose people who have the ability to help you erect desired outcomes.

There's no shame in realizing you are unequally yoked if you reveal it before the actual vowel ceremony. What makes this part difficult is when your differences are being made apparent, but the stakeholders don't have the same concerns about what they both are seeing. When relationships are new, we see the parts we desire to see. We noticed needs being met that have been starved for a very long time. As the relationship matures, and we begin paying attention to the complete picture, we notice things that have always been there, but were obscure before. As time and conversations give way to clarity, perspectives are still being adjusted. There's no set rule on how long this probationary period lasts because you can never determine how long it will take for people to divulge who they truly are.

This is not to say that people aren't honest. My point is, until the picture is clear, you don't know who's standing right in front of you. It's important to know that even the right collaborations have an expiration date. Things that have worked well in the past may not continue to work going forward. That's because people change. Our wants and desires shift, so never assume things will always be what they are now. Put systems in place to help you monitor the status of your partnerships. It's very difficult to have agreement in imagining successes with people you no longer walk in agreement with. When there is a vision for where you're headed, without a plan, the process can be chaotic. It doesn't mean you'll never get there, but what will the collateral damage be once you arrive? Here's the Catch 22. Extremely large visions are rarely realized because of the work of the visionary alone. The visionary needs people to make it happen but may not be a people person. Being unequally yoked is when you connect with people who want what you can do, more than they want you. The bind will only last as long as one tolerates the other. This is understood and accepted in the business world. A handshake to seal a deal is a distant memory. Today, contractual agreements are required in all business affairs. Unfortunately, we can no longer enter personal relationships unwary and naïve. It may not be very romantic to show up on a first date with a wall for separation. Because of how vastly our world has changed, we must be cautious and not share too much too soon.

The marriage I spoke of crumbled after 29 years. What we used to imagine together as one became distorted. When this happens, it's important to know that it's happening. It's extremely painful and it changes everything, but change doesn't have to always be a terrible thing. Whether you caused it or feel a victim of it – embrace the change. Things we've been needing in our lives, must find a way in. In many cases, there must be an exchange. As I'm letting something or someone go, I am simultaneously allowing room for that vacancy to be filled. Believe it or not, this is a very exciting position to be in. It's an opportunity to self-analyze and recalibrate. Perhaps you need to shuffle the furniture and reimagine a new future. What if the way you've been imagining requires the cast of partners who are no longer connected to your vision? Don't be held hostage to old imaginations by people who've jumped ship. Ask God to help you fill those empty places so you can be free to imagine unlike ever before.

It's not always apparent when and what we should let go of. If you've not spent much time around people and situations that stimulate you towards growth, you may be somewhat bewildered. Some situations we entertain for a while, take residence with us - not always for our benefit. Parasitism is a close relationship between species where the parasite lives on or inside the host, causing it some harm and is adapted structurally to this way of life. Unless we are good gatekeepers for nurturing environments, we'll become prey and easily devoured. Take a very close look at your affiliations. Are you always the giver – the one responsible for everyone else's joy? If something is always taking and never giving, it's feeding off you. Leeches, tics, and tapeworms can lengthen and bolster as long as they are connected to their host. Are you supplying life-support to negativity without your expressed consent? It's time to cut ties with things that interfere with our creativity. If forging mutually beneficial friendships is

Dr. John D. McConnell

something you need help with, your primary care physician can direct you to a wealth of resources. Pride is sometimes a hindrance to wellness. Consider that anything short of being whole is not only a hindrance, but an insult to one's pride.

How much bigger could your imagination grow if it was shared by a team? What if the people in your inner circle energized your dream by believing and imagining as one? Imagine You Have It!

CHAPTER 7

ADOPTING A NEW MINDSET

I served on a textbook adoption committee a few times over the years as a public-school teacher. At least every eight years school districts change textbooks for the major subjects taught (Reading, Math, Science, and Social Studies). Information and strategies are consistently evolving. New textbooks are always being drafted in an effort to incorporate the most current/relevant learning trends. If our learning institutions embrace change by swapping teaching curriculums every so many years, surely 'adopting a new mindset' is a relevant topic. I'm not suggesting that your entire way of thinking is flawed. It may be that you simply need to adjust some areas of thought. Knowing your mindset aptitude will require you to run a full diagnostic of how you arrive at the choices you make. To accomplish this, you can either use reflection or true reflection.

REFLECTION

This is where most of us live. We think back to what happened and what we did. How we felt about what occurred plays an enormous role. If the outcome was favorable for us, we viewed it as a win and moved forward. If pain was your prize for the transaction, more than likely you assigned the blame to yourself or someone else as a way to cope and keep living.

TRUE REFLECTION

This is usually not immediate, and can take years to experience. You remember what happened but you question why. What made me choose that way? How did I allow myself to be in that position? How many times have I been here? Was it my fault? Even if the outcome was favorable for you, you still considered the other people involved. Were my actions fair? Did I cause harm? Should I have responded differently?

Maturity should be an all-encompassing maturation. Our age and health should not be the only components. Our thoughts, strategies, patience, tolerance, knowledge, and understanding should all mature as well.

Many people rail against starting over. No matter what it is, starting over is usually not the first consideration. On the surface, it seems like the most labor-intensive option, but actually it takes longer to re-purpose an old version of a thing.

If you can decide to want something, you can have it. I'm not even talking about exercising the strategies for pulling it into your life. Just picturing it as yours is enough to start its journey toward your hands. Think about the things you wanted in your life. How did they come to you? Did they sneak in and then all of a sudden, they were part of your possession? No, it came because you thought of it. You saw it somewhere, heard about it, and gave it air to breathe. It was something about what you did that asked it into your life. Let's peel back the mysteriousness of it all, and add more intentionality to it. Although we've been studying the mind for years, human beings did not create it. For all we know about the power of our mind, imagine how much more we still don't know. Change your mind to change your world. Be careful what you imagine. It just may knock on your door.

GROWTH MINDSET

A growth mindset is essential for continued learning, and builds resilience - essential for accomplishment in all walks of life. A growth mindset chooses to believe that none of the time invested has been wasted. Even if things don't play out exactly as you've imagined, you end up better than you were before. Your starting point tomorrow is much further down the line because you didn't shy away from the work today. This type of mindset is nurtured by patience. Look to Winemakers to appreciate the significance of a growth mindset. They understand that the flavor they're seeking can't be rushed. As a wine's aroma evolves, so does the flavor. Tannins tend to soften over time, making wine feel smoother and more elegant. Cellar-worthy wines are recommended to be aged up to twenty years. At NASA, candidates undergo up to two years of training to become fully qualified astronauts - with no guarantee of ever traveling to space. Teachers, doctors, lawyers, and scientists, all require specialized training that accredits them for their field of work. Many continue the rigorous and extensive path to obtain post-graduate degrees. If goalsetting and time management can get one this far, where can one end up with an uninhibited imagination?

It's hard to appreciate other people's perspectives if you're oblivious to them. When people complain about their voice not being heard, does it irritate you or prompt you to seek resolution for them? If you're irritated by someone not feeling validated, it hints that you are far removed from their reality. There are billions of us under the same restrictions of gravity and oxygen, yet our lifestyles have polar differences. I didn't understand that Kansas City, Kansas was a small place until I moved to Houston, Texas. The information had been shared with me, but it took experiencing it for myself to realize it. Whether it's geography, race, gender, age, or occupation – we will always have opportunities to adjust our mindset. This may seem like a play on words, but having a proper mindset involves action on our part. We must on purpose, set our mind regarding specific things. How I treat my body, my respect towards women, how I honor God, choosing to uphold marital vowels, etc. all require action based on how my mind is set.

I don't think we truly appreciate our differences until we see them up close. One part of the world doesn't experience things the same way as another part. Until you go away to college, serve in the military, or get recruited by a job a thousand miles away from where you were raised, you may never know how the other half lives. Having influence with those you can't relate to is about as difficult as a magician making his audience disappear. Who we are going forward is a direct correlation to how sensitive we are to the people and issues we are surrounded by.

If you (like most) have inherited your belief system, more than likely the way you imagine has also been passed down. To adopt something implies that it's not original - but transferable. Perhaps when it comes to taking the limits off of our imagination, we should go beyond recycling someone else's mindset – to creating a totally new way of engaging our mind!

The imagination can paint a portrait of what's to come just moments before it happens. At times, the mind needs the pressure of the moment to engage it. Notable performers have learned to conjure their imaginations for what they need while on stage. Like magic, prolific vocal stylists and musicians perform error-free riffs and runs they've never practiced. Dancers and athletes have choreographed movements in the very moment with fans in the seats. Songwriters have sat at a piano or with a guitar, and created songs in minutes that the world will sing for the next seventy-five years. It's not a trick, but a gift we were born with that must be unlocked. You can't unlock what you don't understand. I've never been able to open a door I didn't have a key for. Don't view this gift as not being for you. That's what has kept it out of your reach thus far. The lazy part of the brain works to convince the hyperactive part that there's nothing left to discover. Aren't you tired of taking losses in situations you clearly should be winning? Engage your imagination first by acknowledging that it is a very real living part of you. Stop allowing your brain to trick your imagination to underperform.

Our imagination is a weapon to protect us from depression and suicide. The leading culprits of depression in adults are stressful events, personality, family, history, pregnancy and giving birth, menopause, loneliness, alcohol and drugs, and illness. Winning these battles demand that we first win the battle for our mind.

The consensus among leading brain researchers for improving brain function, is that we should exercise regularly, get plenty of sleep, eat a Mediterranean diet to stay mentally active, remain socially involved, and keep our blood vessels healthy. To this list I add, Imagine You Have It.

If you could create a totally new way of engaging your mind, how different would life be? What if you had the keys to unlock your understanding? Would this cause your imagination to flourish? Imagine You Have It!

CHAPTER 8

WANT WHAT YOU WANT

Have you been immersed in life enough to know what you want? We really don't know what we don't know until it's introduced to us. Do yourself a favor each year and plan a trip to go somewhere you've never been. I volunteer for a camp each summer that allows teenagers to experience aquatic and aviation careers up close. These kids get a front row seat, to what it takes to operate the Houston Ship Channel and the Port of Houston. They spend several hours at the

Lone Star Flight Museum and an entire day at Space Center Houston. By the end of a week, we've given their imaginations lots of new things to consider. There is no way to want what you're unaware of. You may feel an emptiness or longing, but until you are able to see it up close or in your imagination, there's no way to know it exists. It's not permission we need to craft our wants, but more insight into ourselves. Things are easily ruled out once you discover what you like. This doesn't mean you must try everything. My point is, when you develop positive attachments to certain things, it's easy to spot what no longer fits. If the way you live resembles that of a packrat, perhaps you should evaluate what's truly important to you and let go of the excess. It's cute to try to live the lives others imagined for us, until it conflicts with our own desires. It's better to have things we're hanging onto, than it is for them to hang onto us.

I have always loved Christmas, but I learned early that my high expectations would not be rewarded. I received nice gifts, and I was grateful, but nothing ever matched what I had imagined. Truth is, it hurt more not to get what I expected, so I began curbing my imagination. I remember feeling embarrassed for wanting so much, knowing that some of my friends were less fortunate than me. It was hard not to want at that level as a kid. We didn't have the internet in the seventies, but it was the era of the JCPenney large general catalogs. During my childhood, JCPenney put out three big book catalogs - in full color every year. Some of them measured a whopping one thousand pages. My siblings and I spent hours flagging all the toys we wanted Santa to bring us. I learned young that I couldn't control my fate, and it was in my best interest to manage my expectations. I think that's where it happens for most people. A series of things occur, and eventually we give up, so our future disappointments won't devastate us as much. Newsflash – you still control the rutter of your ship.

As I mentioned about my youthful Christmas, if there is a downside to imagining things, it would be to not get what you've imagined. Although that's a defeating feeling, it builds character. Don't stop wanting what you want just because there's a chance you may never get it. We can't totally control getting what we want any more than we can control things coming into our lives we would never invite. Alzheimer's, Parkinson's, and cancer are equal opportunity illnesses. Extremely bad things lurk to be on display, that we consider unimaginable. Even when the most unimaginable things occur, we must forecast thoughts beyond the struggle. Those thoughts (imaginations) energize us towards desired outcomes. Of course, illnesses aren't the only negative things we hope not to see manifest in our lives. When we entertain certain conversations, we grant permission for some things to pull up a chair and hang out for a while. Things we ponder can easily become food for thought when we don't seize the moment and shut them down in their infancy. We can't stop thoughts from coming, but they have no right to linger without permission. The very things we meditate on gain viability. What makes them viable is the breath we breathe into them. Unsuspectingly we give our fears an anatomy. As children, we imagine a boogie man in our bedroom closet, or underneath our bed. We assign physical attributes to our monsters, and the next thing you know they have faces. Although we've never seen them naturally, in our mind's eye – we see them every day in our imagination construct. If we're honest, our fears play a role in our nightly routines. Completely closing the closet door, ensuring the nightlight is on, and never reaching under the bed in the middle of the night, are strategies to keep our monsters at bay. What if we took more control over what we imagine? Instead of fearing things, let's change the word to respect. If I adopt a healthy respect for the propensity of things becoming real, then fearing it becomes unproductive. Respect incentivizes me to positive action, whereas fear is crippling and destructive. Between what I fear and what I respect, I am far less likely to face my fears as I am the things I respect. Let's start enjoying more victories as a result of becoming more intentional. Most things don't have an opportunity to simply creep into our lives unsuspectedly. What are you giving breath to? What are you intentionally or unintentionally inviting into your life?

You can't stop at only imagining. Although powerful, the imagination is one of many required sources for pulling excellence into our lives. Acting alone, it will keep us optimistic and hopeful, but why stop there?

At the age of forty-five, I decided to move to Los Angeles, California to pursue a music/acting career. Quitting my job and moving from Houston to LA was a big risk, but the riskier part was that I was moving away from my wife and two kids. Do you realize how sold out you have to be to take potentially family-destroying risks? There were so many reasons why I shouldn't have made the move, but there were too many reasons why I had to take the journey. Being able to imagine myself landing a starring role in a sitcom or movie wasn't enough to make me uproot my life. Your imagination can show you a picture of what your life can be, but it cannot grow legs and walk it out for you. Devising a plan to attain more, or choosing to only have what you've been having will always be an individual choice.

I believe what we ultimately want in life is suppressed beneath our subconscious until certain connections are made. Until we learn who we are, how can we know what we want? Early successes can handicap a person's pursuit for contentment. Financial prosperity is the end of the journey for most people. What if money has always been plentiful in your life? How do you tap into your purpose for living? Parents' expectations don't automatically manifest in their children. We all must arrive at our own place of awakening – where we are triggered to notice that something we need isn't there. Appetites are activated by hunger, and unless you discover your need, no hunt will ensue. To finally understand what you're missing, is almost as liberating as attaining it. The passion to bring it into your life is ignited because your imagination lends you a glimpse of what it can be. As we enter adulthood, our imaginations become flabby and out of shape. Like biceps and triceps, muscles that don't get a lot of activity lose tone and definition. There was a time when a simple thought would suffice as an ember to spark our imagination. Now, we require proof of life before validating the thought.

PUT ON THE COAT

At a certain point, you must put on the coat and begin walking in your newfound privilege. Get over the shock of how things used to be. You know so much more now, and it's not just a coincidence. All of your experiences have pushed you to arrive in the place you now stand. The covenant prize for a golfer is to win The Masters. This particular golf tournament represents golf's most distinguished summit. Not just anyone can sign up to participate. You must qualify. Those who win are presented with a special blazer designed only for members of that fraternity. It separates Masters Champions from everyone else in the room. Not every winner has the same personality. Nevertheless, wearing the coat prevents you from having to speak at all. The coat's reputation and status symbolizes greatness.

The majority of us will never play in a Masters tournament, but greatness is still our path. One of LeBron James's pseudonyms is, "King James", and now and again he gestures as though he's placing a crown on his head. Get in a mirror and see yourself putting on your coat of greatness. You qualify! There are moments when you can feel things shifting in your favor. Don't play it down anymore. Put on the coat! Aren't you tired of asking people if they think you should step out to follow what's in your heart?

If you finally discovered what's been missing from your life, would anything be able to prevent you from pursuing it? If you could imagine again as you did when you were a child, how far would your thoughts take you? Imagine You Have It!

CHAPTER 9

YOU CAN'T FAIL IF YOU DON'T QUIT

What determines failing? If my goal is to pass the bar and become a lawyer, am I a failure just because I didn't pass the test? After being accepted into law school, and completing all of the requirements - the label I'm tagged with is "failure" for not apprehending the ultimate prize? That doesn't seem fair. What about the successes of graduating high school, then college, and being welcomed into a law degree program? Don't short circuit what success truly is. Don't reserve your celebration for the covenant prize. View each step along the way as a moment worthy of praise! Forward progress is not always easy. Even for the same outcome, the journey we all take to get there looks different. If athletes must practice competing at high levels, why would it be different for things non-sports related? Think of your imagination as a form of practice. I must imagine myself piloting a plane, conducting an orchestra, or resecting a bowel long before it ever really happens. Our imagination allows us to test drive a profession to see if the reward matches the sacrifices required. Seeing yourself in the role helps to justify the why. Why pursue something so difficult (time-consuming; arduous)? How each of us answers that question is totally our prerogative, and the very reason we should visualize it first. You're only a failure when you cease to challenge yourself to continue gaining ground. The lessons I learn today should inform the map I chart for tomorrow. I may benefit more from changing my direction, despite the opinions of the majority.

We've been conditioned to believe there's one specific road to take for our success. Even if it's a path someone else selected for you, once you're on it, it's yours. Not so. Life doesn't fit perfectly into compartments that way. We change our minds, have an epiphany, or realize new opportunities. Deviating from one's original path is not considered by all to be a smart decision. At a certain point, we must stop overly concerning ourselves with the opinions of others. Your decision-making may appear erratic to some, but your life is your own. Let's talk about failure from a different perspective. Let's say for years you've invested in becoming more educated, and you learn that you've been operating below your privilege. Should you be considered a failure if you choose to stay the course you're on? I'd rather not stigmatize anyone with that label. But I'm sure you see how an argument can be made for both sides of the coin. Information is power. The more of it we gain, the sturdier our stance can become. What are the things you stand for, and from what information do you base that stance? If you later found your information to be totally inaccurate (misleading, false), would you maintain your same level of support? If someone has interrupted your progress because of imprisoning you with that label, it's time you go free. If you find it hard to separate your relationship with people from their opinions of you, you may need to let those people go altogether.

I grew up in a traditional Baptist church, where we said, 'amen' in response to the preacher, clapped our hands to the rhythm of the music, and sang aloud with the choir. In my late teens, I started visiting a Pentecostal church, where praising God was even more expressive. Over there it was the norm to lift and waive your hands in worship. I noticed it became increasingly harder for me to worship at my home-church because I didn't feel I could be as expressive there as I had become at the Pentecostal church. There was no rule that I couldn't praise God as I desired there. However, I felt it difficult to press past how I knew the congregation had always known me to be during worship. What other people thought was so heavy on my mind, that I eventually had to leave the Baptist Church to feel free enough within myself to worship God the way I felt most comfortable. Whatever you need to do to live life outside of the judgment of others, do it – no matter how silly it seems.

Break out of your old trappings. There is a better way to be a spouse, sibling, parent, friend, etc... Grow to the place of demanding your freedom. If you never fight for it, you'll fade away, dying prematurely. Never experiencing fulfillment but knowing it exists promotes bitterness - which is as contagious as 'whooping cough'. You may be familiar with the saying, "One bad apple can spoil a bunch". That famous phrase is used to illustrate how one person's negative demeanor or bad behavior can affect or perpetuate a negative attitude amongst a whole group of people. Your inability to be satisfied can seep over into the lives of your children in the form of resentment. Relatives, friends, and coworkers tolerate us when we're not at our best, but is that enough? Although we shouldn't go through life seeking approval, how we affect those close to us should be a top concern. How many times will you press the snooze button before fully waking up? Don't stack this book on the shelf with the others. Purpose not to be tolerated but celebrated. You will know you've done the work when it becomes a common practice for you to visualize your actions before making them. Carpenters have a saying – "measure twice; cut once". This simply means you can save time, money, and energy by being one hundred percent sure of your measurement. It costs so much when we get it wrong. If you've gotten it wrong so many times that you literally can't imagine things going the right way, this manuscript is definitely for you. Stop leaving a trail of damage behind your every decision. People connected to you shouldn't have to suffer all because you refuse to count the cost. The distance between getting it right and getting it wrong is usually very subtle. Why are you still doing life the same way? There's obviously a problem. Those who allow themselves to become victims of their mistakes trade-in spouses, friends, business partners, etc. The saying goes, "when you extend your hand to point at someone, three of your fingers are pointing at you". Until we own our ways and visualize better decisions, our results will always be the same.

If your imagination starts to take you on a path you've never seen, follow it. Your knowledge of what's right and wrong will nudge you if things aren't right. But if the journey is positive, there's no way to know its end without continuing. Don't fail yourself by quitting unnecessarily. Always believe the best is yet to come. This will energize you to work towards freedom rather than retirement.

Try viewing your imagination as a friend. Give it an opportunity to earn your trust. What you must remember is, it has no way of going any further than you allow. It can never override you. You have veto power. But your imagination can only show you where it would like you to go. You can't stretch it without sanctioning it to work for you. It's usually not our imaginations we fear, but the residue they leave. When accessed correctly, we see ourselves doing things beyond our power. It may be something we're capable of doing, but at the point your imagination shows you, it's not more than an intuition. The job of our imagination is to get us ready for what could be our reality. The manifestation has nothing to do with the dream itself. That would be like blaming our shoes for making us late for work. The imagination is a tool to support us in getting where we want to go, but not the actual vehicle. We have vilified one of our most effective tools, perhaps at our own peril. Stagnation shows up when our thoughts can no longer forecast happy and joyful times. Put your imagination back in the game. You can't win without it. You must imagine her holding your hand at the altar in a wedding dress before finding the courage to ask her out on a first date. Visualizing your well-toned, muscular body, is what motivates you to get a gym membership. Without envisioning your business thriving, you'll never apply for the loan to get it up and running. Let your imagination do its job. You do the rest.

If you are someone who does not use your imagination, it's not a phase you'll grow out of. There is a block you have set for whatever reason. The imagination is an incredible feature of our consciousness. When we don't use it, it's because we no longer trust it to be beneficial. If you're unable to point to anything your thoughts have assisted you with, perhaps you're right. But is there anything we can do to make something that's low performing, an asset? You may not be clear on why you have little reliance on your imagination. What is clear; however, is until you employ it more, bitterness is in your future. The imagination is a protective factor our brain relies on for stimulation. Although imagining isn't it's only stimulant, it plays a big role in our daily motivation. The alternatives to a healthy imagination can be negative choices, such as drugs and alcohol. Discovering why we may not be yielding to our imagination will help us become more intentional in reincorporating it as a daily practice.

What if your new choices brought you closer to happiness? Would you be excited if your spouse and children saw you as being more considerate? If you could rise above the debris-field of your past mistakes, and make better choices, how awesome would you feel? Imagine You Have It!

CHAPTER 10

WHERE DO WE GO FROM HERE

Can we truly turn back the hands of time, reverting to a childlike gullibility of the world? Will we ever again have an idea that we think is big enough to change the world? If I was a betting man, I'd wager that the majority of you reading this book did not see it as brand-new information, but a reminder of the way you used to be. I am so mad at the circumstances in my life that drastically reduced my ability to dream. I miss the guy who couldn't fall asleep at night because of all of the ideas too large for his imagination to process. I hope these words empower you as they have me, to get back on the path. It's really not as hard as we make it out to be. This isn't something we need a prescription for. The reason we consider success stories as anomalies, is because it gives us an excuse not to exercise our imagination. After you have assigned a meaning, for something stellar happening for someone else, and not for you, are you done? Let that be your ignition source. Stop resenting people for living a life you've lost courage to imagine for. Instead, allow their testimony to remind you of your own possibilities.

Now that we realize we're not simply game pieces on a board, what is our play? Do we continue to be victims of "whatever happens", or do we apply ourselves to determine what's next? Let's move beyond the questions to see just how many things we can answer in our lives. There is no phantom power, calling audibles from behind a curtain. You determine the parameters of your life. You must begin with your thoughts. Employ more discipline to eradicate the negativity always surrounding you. You're not the only one who has bad thoughts. They come to us all, but we must master the art of not taking them. Let's take the advice we give our children when they come home from school crying because someone said mean things to them. "Ignore it". "Stay away from them, and make new friends". "Keep your head up and move on". "You know that's not the truth, and that's all that really matters". Growing older does not nullify the armament formed against us. When we nurture negative thoughts about ourselves, the retreat within us begins.

It's hard to admit shortcomings. No one wants to be defined by areas of weakness. It actually takes strength to acknowledge we have areas that need change. No one alive is without that characterization. When we confront these areas, we realize that they don't actually define us. They are not who we are, but where we are in the moment. Not to be offensive, but those who peruse pornography are attempting to use their imagination to be casted in scenes very different from their reality. This is typically what we do in every situation where we lack confidence. Unless or until we learn how to imagine it differently, we simply act as though it's not our issue. How is that working for you? Not owning it delays the inevitable. We kick it down the road hoping it will never be in the spotlight. The thing we all know is, even if everyone is not aware, it's a problem because you know about it. How safe would you feel building a house next to an inactive volcano? Our best intentions can't protect us from behaviors

 Dr. John D. McConnell

we choose not to acknowledge or rectify. We must assume that a volcano at some point will do what volcanoes do.

Where do you feel most comfortable, in your thought life, or in the real world? Most people I encounter prefer the company of themselves to being in large groups. Although we're always being judged, there is a feeling of safety when we keep things 'close to the vest'. You may have heard the high statistics of men who choose not to see a doctor. Follow the logic or lack thereof. If they have a bad illness, like cancer, they'd rather not know. The financial, physical, and mental burden of treatment feels as much like death as the balance of the disease. These are usually men with the history of heartache and failure. Hope in the past has proven futile, so why should they expect anything different? We typically expect what we are conditioned to expect. These men don't want to die from an illness, but they've watched so much be taken from so many. After you figure out why you think that way, is it ok to stay there? Hell no! Our personalities play a huge part in how we choose to live. What's comfortable for me may not closely resemble what's comfortable for you. Choosing where to go from here may require a compromise between what's always been comfortable and what is best for me.

It becomes increasingly difficult to inspire us to greatness. The tricks have been played, and now we see the weapons for what they are. Stop responding politely to the degenerating rhetoric. Identify it quickly so you can immediately change the setting (radio station, TV channel, friends, business partners, etc.). Negative thoughts and comments are as debilitating as quicksand. The imagination you need to kickstart the best version of you, can only be grown in positive soil. When people want more for us than we want for ourselves, it never translates into a winning formula. A pinch hitter cannot affect the change we desire to see. Coaches and consultants are excellent resources, but ultimately, I am the ship's rudder. I must recognize the need for change, identify the tools required, and realize the ability is within me. Thinking ourselves happy must become something we believe we are worthy of. Sadly, many people don't believe it's their right to be happy. That's my entire purpose for writing this book. Everyone deserves to be fulfilled, and what that looks like, for each of us must be imagined FIRST! We must FIRST imagine friendships where respect, love, and kindness are reciprocal. FIRST imagine careers that are purpose-driven, and financially bountiful. FIRST imagine our children as God's heritage. When we allow our world to be crafted by our best imaginations, then we can truly enjoy the journey of making it our reality.

Imagining it first chokes away fear, and injects hopeful anticipation for what's to come. Stop settling. Imagine beyond the risks, so you're empowered to always chase your dreams.

Can we really call using our imagination, taking a risk? People have said there's no such thing as a sure win. I totally disagree. You lose nothing by engaging your imagination. Many risks millions have taken are associated with making life-altering decisions without the benefit of filtering them through the lens of the mind. How can you know you want something if you've never seen it before? Risky behavior is having unprotected sex with multiple partners, or buying a house you've never physically laid eyes on. Some people detest buying clothes they've not had an opportunity to try on. To imagine something for your life is not a guarantee for a perfect fit, but it is definitely not risky behavior. In fact, those things we failed to consider or imagine as possibilities, can be the cause of many years of struggle. Nothing occurs in life without a cause. "Cause and Effect" is a principle we can't violate anymore than the law of gravity or the law of electrical forces. If you are a phenomenal singer, but choose to never ever share your voice, that gift becomes inconsequential. With your choice, you nullify the potential of anyone being soothed by your songs. Your choice guarantees that you'll never record a solo album, or be nominated for a Grammy. You choosing not to sing certifies that you will never sell-out a colosseum or go on tour as a singer. It's not enough for things we're good at to choose us. Unless we choose them back, we can never experience the effect we should be making. Imagine that!

To cope with the stress of his mother's chronic health issues, young Jim Carey spent hours making funny faces in front of a mirror in his room. He later became famous for developing a talent for impressions. Though plagued with alcoholism and drug abuse, Stephen King authored critically acclaimed books, like "Misery" and "The Green Mile". He was said to have banged out the entire 400-page novel, "Cujo", during a weekend. Imagination alone won't put your talents on display, but it is a very important piece of the puzzle.

We go up from here – to heights we previously never gave ourselves permission to fathom. From here, we go out – way beyond the lines drawn by others to limit us. With what we now know, we go through – penetrating every wall intended as a barrier.

Although it may seem your imagination has departed, it will never leave you all alone. Like any meaningful relationship, you can only get out of it what you put in. Keep a journal to track the exploits of you and your imagination. Begin writing down the expectations you have for yourself, your children, your business, and your relationships. Date your entries and include some strategies you think will assist you in meeting your goals. Every six months or so, revisit what you've written down. You may be shocked to see the progress you've made. There is no competition between you and your imagination. It's part of you. You are it and it is you.

What if you could admit that you have behaviors you don't fully understand, but would like to change? How far could you excel if you decided to embrace the importance of visualizing things prior to calling them into your life? Imagine You Have It!

CHAPTER 11

ACCESS GRANTED

The word "imagination"(or it's synonyms) appears 196 times in this book - so my focus is not subtle. Starting right now at this very moment, you are empowered to begin your new journey. There is no application to complete, or any educational requirements. No one has an advantage or head-start you must contend with. You are equipped and prepared to access your new consciousness. It's new because of your outlook. Your keen awareness of how and why our imagination serves us, allows you further entrance into it. Because you now know the kind of help you need from your imagination, you can better harness its power.

Take full advantage of the benefits package. A few years ago, I joined a gym without the pleasure of having a tour. My purpose for joining was to utilize the treadmills, swimming pool, hot tub, and steam room. Each time I went to workout, I discovered a new amenity I knew nothing of. After two months, I went to the front desk and asked for a complete tour of everything included in my membership. I was astonished by the number of services available to me that I hadn't yet tapped into. Sometimes a simple explanation of benefits is enough to arouse a whole new perspective.

Give your imagination assignments with due dates. Procrastination has been the enemy to productivity for so long. No longer allow your imagination to stroke your ego and convince you that you have plenty of time. Lots of things said about time are untrue, like "Time heals all wounds". The time quotes I embrace are, "Lost time is never found again.", "Time waits for no one.", and "Better three hours too soon than a minute too late". Our imaginations are so incredible, that if unchecked, they could lull us into a slump of inactivity. Once you know what you want to accomplish, put pressure on your thoughts to bring it in.

Pay attention to your standards for living so you can adjust them accordingly. We tend to live based on the measurements others use. Have you noticed how equality is structured in the workplace? Traditionally, people are grouped by salary. In an office where ten or more people share the same job title, their salaries are usually similar. It's difficult to work alongside someone doing the same job as you, making mountains more than you. HR sets salaries to keep coworkers competitive with one another. It's ok for you to make slightly more than me as long as I have a path to also reach that level. This system only works if all the players continue to play along. What if you chose to display a work ethic unmatched by any of your peers, or if your quality of work exceeded anything you've ever seen? Not only would that obliterate the formula for competitive salaries, but would clearly show a massive distinction. Destroy the template by moving to the beat of your own drum. Move out of the box most people are imprisoned by and set a new standard, that only your imagination can show you.

There are doors of opportunity our imagination can open to us, that our character will destroy. Our creative ideas and special skills make us noticeable, but if we have a cruel and demeaning personality, people will choose to go the other way. What a shame it would be to reengage the power of your imagination while forsaking good character and integrity. Our imagination can get people to look our way. Your social skills will determine if it's more than a glance. If you've tasted defeat for the better part of your life, you may not be aware when you're walking in bitterness. Depending on the environments you've been a part of, you may consider lashing out a protective factor. Let's purpose to leave who we were where we were. That's not to say that we should abandon who we are. But be intentional that your actions reflect who and where you are right now. Don't be callous towards people you've only just met. They are not responsible for the pain others caused you.

Just like character, the same can be said for bodily exercise, diet, and many other good practices vital for a healthy being. Don't substitute one important component for another. Finding a way to include your imagination as part of a regular routine will support the balance your life may be lacking.

When I decided to write this book, there was no assumption that the human imagination is failing. It works well for so many. Apparel, cosmetics, cuisines, automobiles, and entertainment are all manifestations of thriving imaginations. I began paying attention to myself and realized my ability to imagine had dwindled. I discovered it was affecting my quality of life, and I began wondering why.

It is estimated that the global number of suicides per year is just under eight hundred thousand people. My deductive reasoning says that at least eight hundred thousand people every year are unable to imagine a world that has them in it. That's a problem! I wrote this book to affect that number. Every life is worth living, and you must begin imagining living well!

Incorporating positive tips for accessing your mind's creative thoughts alone will not magically make life feel better. Becoming disgusted with life took some time, and so will falling in love with it all over again. At the very least, allow this book to prime the pump – whetting your appetite for vivid dreams that will rock your world. Perhaps you've been waiting your whole life for your purpose to be revealed. Choose a path and dare your imagination to get involved. You must couple what it shows you with expectation. Our expectations determine our reality. What is a diet, rehearsal, job interview, a gym membership, or a date without expectation? It's the reason we do things or choose not to. I invest nothing in the things of which I have no expectation. If I believe the fruit of the endeavor is a bust, then I won't endeavor at all. Unless there is an expectation of good, there is nothing to motivate our acceleration of energy. Positive or negative, expect anything fueled by the right source to grow. There are fires on record that have burned for 7 1/2 weeks (fifty-two days). Feed anything what it needs to survive and it will thrive. Doubt and fear perpetuate doubt and fear. How long would hope burn within us if we decided to feed it? If you forever doubt your ability to live out what your mind shows you, you'll never see the manifestation. We are empowered to imagine greater things down the line, as we put our hands to the tasks of today. When we're finally able to hold it in our hands, our imagination says, "Let's do it again".

Are you ready to feed your hope? It's time to walk through the doors of your imagination and experience another level of living.

Aren't you ready to abolish the slavery of your mind and finally be free? The keys are in your hand. Access granted!

IMAGINE YOU HAVE IT!

Dr. John D. McConnell

THE PURPOSE OF THE BOOK COVER DESIGN

A Ruby signet ring symbolizes power, prestige, and style. It is a timeless piece of jewelry associated with love, passion, and authority for thousands of years. The ark over the heart of a king's ring, symbolizes the provision and protection of God, which never fails to cover us. The diamond heart represents our hearts which are precious, beautiful, and to be cherished like diamonds.

Traditionally, signet rings were worn on the pinky finger and used as a seal to sign important documents engraved with the family crest. The signet ring would be dipped into hot wax before being used to print a signature. Pinky rings worn on your dominant hand represent achievement and success, and can serve as a reminder of inner strength, confidence, and the pursuit of one's dreams and ambitions. While you're working to positively expand your imaginations, symbolically wear a pinky ring to assist you in imagining you have it!

ABOUT THE AUTHOR

DR. JOHN DAVID MCCONNELL

Dr. John David McConnell is the owner of Prolyric Productions Publishing Company. Born and raised in Kansas City Kansas, John received his Bachelor of Science degree at Saint Mary College in Leavenworth, Kansas. John taught grades 2 through 8 over the span of his 27-year career as a public-school educator. 20 of those years were with the Houston Independent School District.

In 2016 John received his doctorate in sacred music from Christian Bible Institute & Seminary. His war chest of badges includes Christian, father of two sons, educator, actor, singer, songwriter, worship-leader, Certified Christian Counselor, and author. John exited his teaching career in 2022, and is currently pursuing his literary and songwriting careers full-time.

To Contact John McConnell:
Johndmac4@aol.com
832-865-0260